HYPERGROWTH

How the **customer-driven** model is revolutionizing the way businesses build products, teams, and brands

By: David Cancel, co-founder & CEO of Drift

Foreword by: Hiten Shah, co-founder of KISSmetrics, Quick Sprout, & Crazy Egg

Editor: Dave Gerhardt
Designer: Erik Devaney

Foreword

A former competitor reveals his secrets

Back in 2010, David Cancel and I were friends.

Then he pivoted his company and became my direct competitor.

At the time, I was the CEO of KISSmetrics, a web analytics company I founded back in 2008. David, meanwhile, was the CEO at Performable, which specialized in marketing automation software

When I learned that David was adding web analytics to Performable's feature set, and that he'd now be competing directly with me and my company KISSmetrics, I was frustrated. But not for the reasons you might think.

It's frustrating to compete against David because he doesn't cut corners. And he'll never take the easy way out.

He won't offer a 50% discount to take your customers away. He won't trash you and your product behind your back.

What he will do, is go out and build a better product. And over time, he'll serve his customers better than you're serving your customers. His customer-driven approach will always win out in the end.

I learned a number of valuable lessons from watching David operate in the same space for a year, and I continued to learn from him after he sold Performable to HubSpot in mid-2011.

Going into 2011, HubSpot's churn rate was getting too high and its growth was decelerating. David came in, restructured the engineering team, and rebuilt the product.

That was not an easy job to do at HubSpot's scale, having pulled in $15M+ in 2010.

In 2012, HubSpot rebounded under David's product leadership. They cut churn in half and more than doubled their LTV:CAC ratio.

From there, as Jason Lemkin observed, "they accelerated faster than the average SaaS company to IPO."

At HubSpot, David didn't come in and simply add a new sentence to the company mission statement. He made fundamental changes to the way the team was structured and the way it was operating.

What made it work was David's rapid execution and his learning behind the scenes that builds up conviction for his decision-making.

When he finds what he's looking for, he doubles down hard and fast on the decision. Once his mind is made up, his business is operating that way, his company is operating that way, and his team is operating that way.

As a result, David has become nothing less than one of the very best product leaders in SaaS, and every SaaS founder can learn something from David about how to build a great product and a great business.

In his new book, David finally takes all of his best lessons and his best frameworks and gathers them all in one place.

As a former competitor, it's satisfying to now be able to peek inside of David's mind and see how his customer-driven model was working behind the scenes.
In addition to telling the story of how David took the customer-driven idea he developed at Performable, scaled it at HubSpot, and is now perfecting it at Drift, this book offers a ton of practical and tactical advice for making your company more customer-driven.

Of course, David is always learning and always iterating as a businessperson. So after you're finished reading, stay tuned: I'm sure he'll have more wisdom to share soon.

Hiten Shah
*co-founder of KISSmetrics,
Quick Sprout, & Crazy Egg*

Table of Contents

Introduction

As a college student, I was bored...

Extremely bored.

So I tended to skip all my classes and hang out in the library, where the computers had early versions of the Mosaic browser, and later, the Netscape browser.

Up until this point I had been coding software. Desktop software. Boring software.

I wasn't really feeling it. I didn't love it.

So when I discovered this way to have access to all of this information around the world, and to make connections with people all around the world, I became obsessed. And I started building my first website.

Back in the day, you would put your email address at the bottom of your site. So that's what I did. And eventually, someone sent me a message.

I still remember it to this day:

"Hey man, I really like your website. It's really cool."

Then I checked the IP address: the person who had emailed me was in Russia.

While this interaction might not seem like a big deal, it was actually a breakthrough moment for me. Because it was the first time I had ever experienced a customer feedback loop.

And that is what I've been chasing ever since: that customer feedback loop, and those 1:1 interactions.

While the companies I've founded over the years – including Compete (acquired by WPP), Ghostery (acquired by Evidon), and Performable (acquired by HubSpot) – have all been different, they've all had the same underlying focus:

The connection between businesses and their customers.

I didn't realize it at the time, but I've been chasing that same pattern for nearly 20 years.

Up until my fourth company (Performable), however, I had been following the same playbook as everybody else. And it's a playbook that's largely driven by the ideas and motivations of internal stakeholders.

Whether the underlying methodology is Waterfall, or Agile, the customer is noticeably missing.

At Performable, I shifted the model to make communication with customers a priority.

Under this new model, everything revolves around the customer: from what features get shipped, to how teams are structured, to what words get used on the website.

When Performable was acquired by HubSpot in 2011 and I came in as Chief Product Officer, I had the opportunity to see if my customer-driven approach could work at scale.

Now, at my new company Drift, our mission is to help all companies become more customer-driven.

I believe that in today's world, helping is the new selling and customer experience is the new marketing. Companies that fail to adapt, and that fail to listen to and communicate with their customers, will inevitably lose out.

Centralized planning, Agile, ignoring customers... sure, those things work for slow-growth companies.

But if you're anything like me, you're not interested in slow growth, you're after HYPER-GROWTH.

The customer-driven approach is how you get there.

In this book, I tell the full story of how I developed my customer-driven model, and I share advice and frameworks for helping you implement it at your own organization.

David Cancel

co-founder & CEO of Drift

Chapter 1

The Age of Waterfall & Agile Is Over

I grew up in the age of Waterfall and Agile, and those methods were great for a certain period of time. But the world has changed.

Think about the way you communicate with your friends, family, and co-workers today versus three to five years ago I bet a lot of that communication is now happening over messaging. The shift happened so fast you probably didn't even notice it.

The same thing is happening to businesses. They haven't noticed the shift yet.

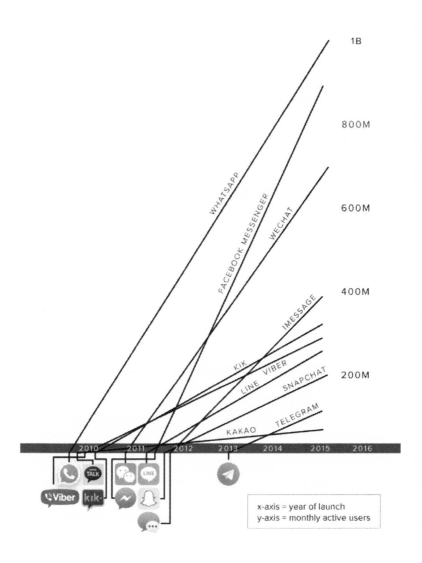

x-axis = year of launch
y-axis = monthly active users

Just look at the numbers: Messaging has exploded, new generations are focused on 1:1 communication by default, and artificial intelligence is finally coming so we can deliver on 1:1 at scale.

Billions of people have already shifted their day-to-day communication. But businesses are stuck in a fields, properties, spreadsheets, and database paradigm. It's a paradigm that has already shifted under our feet.

The new paradigm revolves around messaging and conversations. And the future of business software will be built around that paradigm from the ground up.

Agile and Waterfall were created in an era when communicating with customers and getting feedback was hard. Those approaches made sense in a context where you had no connection with your customer (because you were shipping a product that got installed or put in a box).

But now, communicating with customers and getting feedback has never been easier. And with the rise of SaaS and the on-demand economy, customer expectations have changed.

Customers expect their voices to be heard.

Look at companies like Kickstarter and Indi-egogo, which let people build products out in the open, with the customer.

There's now a growing trend where customers pay for products long before those products even exist.

Take Tesla's Model 3, for example, which racked up nearly 400,000 orders more than a year before its launch.

Customers find value in being part of a community, and being part of that journey of creating the product.

With Agile and Waterfall, customers are left out.
Because customers don't operate in six-week release cycles.

And they don't think about weekly sprints.

And they definitely don't want to hear that the

solutions to their problems are "on the road-map for next quarter."

Think about it: With so many options and competing products available to your customers, do you honestly think customers are going to stick around until you fix that bug in your next release cycle in six weeks?

So, what's the alternative?

At Drift, we've developed a new approach to building products that adds the customer back into the equation. It's called Responsive Development (RD).

RD is based on a set of principles that I've been battle-testing since my Performable days:

Customer-Driven: Always gather first-hand feedback, not second-hand feedback. Get engineers and designers talking directly to customers.

Flexible: RD is based on principles, not rules. Rules are binding. Principles favor progress and forward momentum.

Iterative: Your first attempt will always be imperfect or wrong in some way. The goal is to iterate towards the best possible solution, not try to get it on the first try.

Focused: Iterations should be focused, self-contained, and have as few dependencies as possible.

Rapid: Speed gives you more opportunities to iterate and, therefore, more opportunities to learn.

Incremental: The power of progression and step-by-step improvements lead to better results.

Objective: RD favors data over internal opinion. Results should be measurable and more highly regarded than internal opinions.

Ever-evolving: Learning is never done. Principles will change overtime.

In order to implement Responsible Development at Drift, we created a framework that we call Burndown.

Agile vs. Burndown

	Agile	Burndown
Measure of success	Thoroughness of story, agile points and velocity	End user feature adoption & retention
Means of determining prioritization	Product backlogs and sprint planning	End-user validated design mockups and prototypes.
Speed	Story-based sprints (weeks)	Micro-sprints (days)
Release focus	Multiple features grouped into a single version release	A single version of a single feature per release
Flexibility	2-week sprints are planned, executed & generally inflexible once agreed upon	Every day priorities change and so do the current and upcoming sprints

This new approach to creating and improving products allows us to provide maximum value to our customers.

Because ultimately, every company is here to serve customers.

When you spend more time talking to "internal stakeholders" than your customers, you've lost the ship. That's the truth. It's a failure that can sneak up on you.

It's taken me years to figure all of this out.

In Chapter 2, I'll tell the story of how I stumbled onto the customer-driven model in the first place.

Chapter 2

An Accidental Discovery

In 2009, I started a company called Performable. We were very early in the lean startup world and I used to give a lot of talks at lean startup conferences at the time.

As a product team, we were really focused on the front side of things, which is the customer development side. The customer-driven side was a natural progression

At Performable, we had the same problem in the early days that all software companies have. A product manager or myself would try to convince an engineer that we had to do x, or y, or that we had to fix this thing.

Of course, engineers are usually skeptical, like myself, and they would push back and say it was going to take too long and this and that.

But organically what just happened was -- because we had more customers than we had employees -- everyone at the company, including every engineer, had to do support. And that ended up being a breakthrough moment for us.

We had started the company around this customer-development process and trying to get to product/market fit. Then we got to a point when we did get to product/market fit and, because of our size, we accidentally stumbled into this thing where all of us as a team, around 20 people, were doing support and supporting the customers directly.

This was not easy for traditional engineering teams because engineers typically don't like spending their days talking to customers. But we did it out of necessity. And we considered it a part of our customer development process that we were going through at the time.
The results were amazing.

All of a sudden, the things that we were trying to get engineers to do, to convince them of, they were doing on their own. And they were doing them immediately. It would take 5 minutes where they usually would've argued for weeks about how hard something was going to be, and how they would have to re-architect this, and so on.

So we started to ask them, "Why did you do that?"

And they'd say, "Oh, well I talked to three customers and they all had this problem, so I went in and fixed it."

To a marketer, who was our customer, this blew their minds. Because engineers almost never want to build things for marketers. They definitely don't want to listen to them in-house, or even when they hire them outside. So having our engineers listen to their issues directly, and provide immediate solutions, helped us develop a ton of goodwill.

(We still have old customers from back then who, to this day, say their favorite thing was that any time they would chat with us or call us, our answer to everything was, "Hit refresh," and their issue was fixed.)

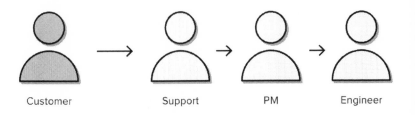

Customer feedback, the traditional way

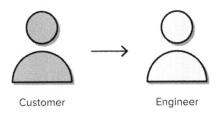

Customer feedback, the customer-driven way

The more that I watched the engineering team hearing directly from the customer, and the faster I saw them responding to the customer and doing things that, in the past, would've taken a lot of drugs deals and arm twisting and cajoling to get them to do, the more I realized that we were onto something.

Our engineers now had the autonomy and the freedom to go and solve problems that they were hearing about directly.

So we started to build a methodology (that's a fancy word, it was less than that) around this thing -- around building really small teams and having them all linked to the customer.

This wasn't some grand strategy or idea, just a way of working that we had stumbled upon.

Chapter 3

Does It Scale?

In 2011, Performable was acquired by HubSpot, a fellow Boston marketing software company.

I knew the team at HubSpot, and I knew their investors, and I knew we wanted the same thing and were headed in the same direction. So we merged. And I went on to lead product at HubSpot as CPO.

Product was a little different at HubSpot, as I owned not only product management, but also design, engineering, and the operations it took to serve up the product.

I built that team from about 50 people to

around 200 by the time I left, which was a few weeks before we went public. (I left with one of my VPs of engineering, and we went off to start a new company, Drift.)

For the 3.5 years I spent leading product at HubSpot, I got to experiment and see if the approach we used at Performable with 20 people could work at scale. We got to cycle it, and refine it, and the short net-net of it is that at HubSpot, we built the most amazing and productive product team that I've ever worked with

The Three-Person Team

We built everything at HubSpot around having an engineering-led organization. And we built the engineering teams around this idea of being small and autonomous.

I have the classic issue enterprenuer issue that I don't like being told what to do. I like to be autonomous. So I started to think, how do we build teams so they are as autonomous as possible? Mostly because that's how I would like to work, and also because I selfishly didn't want to manage a lot of people.

So I just made it up at one point: We're going to have engineering teams that have three people.

It was arbitrary. I made it up.

But of course, everything arbitrary drives engineers crazy. So when I said that all engineering teams were going to be three people in size, they asked: "Why three?"

And I told them: "Because I made it up. It's a starting point. We can refine from there."

So we started with three, and then tested all different kinds of sizes: five-person engineering teams, seven-person engineering teams. We tried all of these different sizes but kept coming back to three.

The three-person engineering team ended up working because it was so small that a tech lead could manage the two other engineers on a team without devolving into becoming a full-time manager.

With just two people to manage, tech leads

could spend 80% to 90% of their time (if not more) coding.

The small team size also meant that everyone on a team could sit together. As a result, most teams did away with traditional meetings and daily standups. They didn't need them. They were sitting together and working together and communicating on an ongoing basis.

Engineer   Tech Lead   Engineer

The three-person team

So we had these three-person engineering teams. And the core thing for each engineering team was that the engineers had to own a complete, customer-facing product -- from the presentation of that product, down to the operation of that product, to the support of that product.

That meant if the product went down in the middle of the night, the engineers were the ones getting paged. It didn't go to a third-party, like an overnight team or a different team within the company. They owned it completely. They owned the QA of their product, they owned the release engineering of their product, and they owned the user testing of their product.

We paired up each of these three-person engineering teams with a product manager, who would usually work across many of these three-person teams. Then for each PM we had a dedicated designer. And we had a product marketing manager who was dedicated as well.

Now, in a typical environment, a PM would inevitably regress into doing a lot of project management work for the engineers, whether that be creating lists, or creating processes, or Gantt charts -- whatever they were doing, they were creating all this process overhead for the engineers.

In order to scale, we needed the engineering

teams to own the solutions. And that included how they built the product, whether they focused on bugs, or features, or what have you, but also how they wanted to project manage that product.

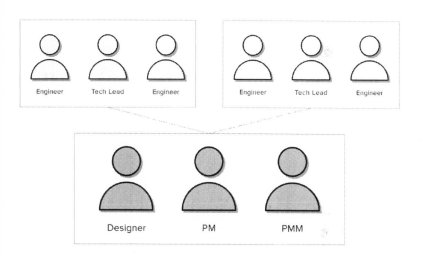

The customer-driven product team

The PM owned the customer, and working with the designer and PMM, and getting out in front of the engineering team and iterating and prototyping and getting feedback from the customers.

All of these people -- the PM, the designer, and the PMM, as well as the engineering teams they were working with -- all sat together. We made sure to co-locate them all as a way to avoid a lot of overhead, and a lot of meetings.

Because when you're sitting next to the people on your team, overhearing what's happening, you know exactly what's going on and can jump in to solve problems that you see emerging, as opposed to waiting to have those problems bubble up to you through a meeting or through some other high-overhead kind of process.

The goal was to increase the amount of ownership, freedom, and autonomy that the teams had, and it was also the glue that made this whole thing work. It allowed the people closest to the problem to come up with the solutions and test those solutions with the actual customer.

After all, those are the people who are spending more time with the customer than anyone else in the company -- more than the executive team, more than the CEO. They have the right perspective in solving this problem and measuring whether they solved the problem or not.

So that's how product, from a structural standpoint, worked at HubSpot. And for a long time the organization was pretty flat. We didn't have hierarchy on top of those teams.

Then, over time, really toward when we started to get toward the 200-person phase, we added a second VP of engineering, and a director. But they were focused primarily on recruiting and on supporting the individual contributors on the team.

Our model was always the servant leadership model, meaning the higher your title, the lower you are on the totem pole -- and the more your job is to support the individual contributors and the customers above you.

Getting Buy-in

In order to get company-wide buy-in for our customer-driven approach, we needed to have transparency and accountability alongside autonomy.

There is no autonomy without accountability. That's something totally different -- that's anarchy, not autonomy.

So all the teams were accountable and transparent about the metrics they were driving toward, and the work that they were doing.

And by doing that, little by little, that's how you gain the support of the internal customers you have, whether that's management, customer service, customer success, sales, marketing -- you get all of their buy-in.

One thing that we did that really helped was that each of those three-person teams -- as well as the PMs, designers, and PMMs -- had metrics that measured them not only on the success of their external customers, but also on the success of their internal customers (e.g. management, customer service, customer success, etc.).

And there were point people across the organization that worked with product to make sure we hit our internal goals.

For example, the team working on the email

product would have this set of customer-facing metrics, and then they'd have this set of internal metrics that they were trying to move with their counterparts: this person right over here in support, and this person right over here of in sales, and this person who's in marketing.

And all of those people would report on the internal customer metrics as well.
So we made it a shared system.

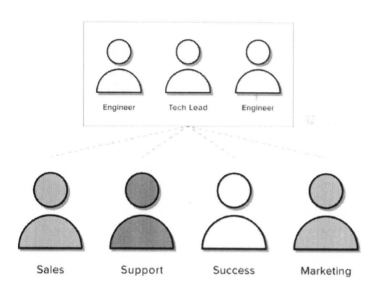

Internal customers

At first it sounds simple, but you can imagine it's not simple to roll out. It takes time to see that it's working and to get buy-in.

But as long as things are transparent, and you have that shared accountability, it buys you a lot of freedom. And it bought us the freedom not to have things like roadmaps and version numbers and dates -- things that are all in the traditional product management world.

The way I think about it, so many of those things are company problems. Those are not customer problems. Our roadmap is not a customer problem ... even though you might hear that from sales

Getting Rid of Roadmaps

Customers care about being heard, and they care about having their feedback taken into account and knowing that something is being done because of that. They don't care about when the next version of your product is coming out.

And that's where we focused in on that philosophy of giving teams ultimate autonomy -- it allowed for the speed and agility necessary to evolve our product as our customers asked for new features and functionality.

Customer needs will inevitably change over time, which means your product will need to change too

There is no real end-goal. The end-goal is evolution.

So at HubSpot I made the decision to not set a public product roadmap. For a company that values transparency, it was a decision that led to a fair amount of handwringing from those wanting a reliable way of knowing what was coming next.

The problem with product roadmaps, however, is that they often satiate company curiosity more than they solve customer problems. I'll give you an example.

Let's say as part of a public roadmap we commit to creating a certain app or feature. Once stated, the completion of that app becomes the end-goal. The sales team previews it. The business readies for it. But then in talking with customers and testing, let's say we discover that the app doesn't solve the problem at all. It's a false approach.

We've then got a dichotomy of needs on our hands. Do we serve the company who in stating it publicly has built up an appetite to see this app in the wild? Or do we serve the customer, abandon the approach and build the thing that's actually going to work?

Roadmaps solve for the company not the customer. What solves for the customer is non-stop testing and a continuous improvement.

In place of a roadmap, the CEO and I would get together once a year and come up with themes for the next year. Not a roadmap, but very high-level themes -- like, "We would like to get into this business, or this area, or deal with this problem." It wasn't. "We need a product that can do x, y, and z," it was asking the question, "Is there a product here?"

I would then communicate those themes to the different product teams, and we would figure out goals for each of the teams on how they would try to drive toward including the themes for the year.

After that, all I cared about was looking at the metrics day-to-day to make sure they were all talking to customers, interacting with customers, releasing frequently, and that customers were -- both from a qualitative and quantitative measure -- getting happier and using the product more frequently.

We also made sure retention was going up over time for the different customer types, for the different cohorts, and for the different plan sizes that we looked at. We looked at it every which way but Sunday.

We had 15 thousand customers at that point, so we could really slice and dice and look at all of those metrics. And as long as those things were moving, we knew we were on the right track.

With a 200-person team, a lot of intervention has to happen to make sure that when people get off course they get back on course. That's all that mattered. The teams came up with their own timelines.

The only thing that I pushed for was that they shipped as soon as possible. And so my answer to everything was either "No," or, "Just ship it."

The Art of Saying No

In the early days at HubSpot, we'd have a lot of pushback about wanting to introduce more and more process into the system. And I'd have to say "No," again and again.

For example, someone would say, "Oh, we need an infrastructure team because of this shared backend thing."

And I'd say, "No."

And they'd ask, "Well who's going to do that?"

And I'd say, "The teams have to do that."

And they'd say, "But the teams also own the customer-facing product."

And I'd say, "Correct."

And they'd say, "Oh, so we have to do that too? But wouldn't it be more efficient if we had a dedicated team that did instrafature so that we could have shared services?"

We used hundreds of microservices at HubSpot, so the idea of having one group focus on infrastructure made sense ... theoretically. But in practice, no. Because teams like that are not connected to the customer. So they tend to drift into projects and into time spans that need a lot of overhead, a lot process, and a lot of management.

And a lot of those projects never end up making it. That 6-month rewrite, or, "We just have to rebuild this part of the structure and it'll be 10 times faster," it never works that way in practice.

So for us, our discipline was that we were going to be customer-focused, and everyone had to be building something that a customer could use.

If we had shared points, which we had hundreds if not thousands of, then we were going to make sure that the different engineering teams were communicating. And that part, the communication part, is the one that would come up all the time.

For example, an engineer would say, "We need to hire a project manager."

And I'd say, "No."

And they'd say, "But I don't know what Michael is working on."

And I'd ask, "Did you talk to Michael?"

And they'd say, "No."

And I'd ask, "Why not?"

And they'd say, "That doesn't scale. I can't talk to Michael. I'm busy. I'm working on my product and this and that."

And I'd say, "No, go talk to Michael."

And they'd say, "Well, Michael is in the Ireland office."

And I'd say, "So send Michael an email."

And they'd say, "He's not going to read it."

So I'd say, "Oh, well look right here, Michael posts every week on the internal wiki -- all the stuff that he's working on. Look it's right here. Have you read this?"

And they'd say, "No I don't have time. The wiki's a mess. I can't search it."

It was almost comical. It would just keep on going.

I had this conversation hundreds of times with engineers, and at the end of the day, I'd just tell them, "No, we're not going to introduce a project manager just because you refuse to talk to someone."

Just ship it.

I used to say this over and over and over. In our HipChat room (this was before we moved over to Slack) you could type in "Just ship it" and a rotating picture of my head would show up.

The phrase has become so ingrained in HubSpot culture that it's now a mural in their new office.

Photo of mural at HubSpot's new office

I was saying "Just ship it" all the time because I wanted the teams to ship daily. And I eventually got to the point where our teams were shipping 500 to 600 times every single day. That was the cadence we were moving out. Instead of having two to three releases per month, we had thousands.

Instead of building up a release for months, we got it into the hands of beta users immediately (often before a HubSpot executive had seen it) so that the customer could help us correct and iterate on our direction.

The most amazing part of all of this was just looking at the results that it drove.

HubSpot, and now Drift, have super high-performance cultures, which means there's not much tolerance for things that don't work, even though they might sound nice.

So the proof of this new approach was in the results, and those were results we saw directly from customers as well as results from within the teams themselves.

After implementing the customer-driven product model at HubSpot, our product team had the highest employee NPS score of any team in the company by a considerable margin, and -- at a time when every engineer and UX designer on the planet had a million job offers -- our team's employee retention rates were off the charts.

Chapter 4

What It Takes to Achieve HYPERGROWTH

Everyone in your company needs to be communicating with customers continually, and in different forms. Some of that is in-person, some of that is via live chat, some of that is via Skype, some of that is via a Slack group, and some of that is answering support questions via email or even on the phone.

At Drift, there are lots of ways we are communicating with customers. But communicating alone isn't enough: We've also made sure our internal incentives are aligned with our goal of serving the customer.

We set up all of our metrics internally -- both for the engineering and product teams, as well as across the entire company -- to be metrics that are proxies for customer success.

That way, if we're looking at these metrics, and they look solid, we know the teams are going in the right direction.

This accountability to the customer has allowed us to build a culture at Drift that gives the teams -- especially the engineering, product, and design teams -- pretty much complete autonomy in deciding what they're working on, and when they're working on it.

Are they working on new features? Bugs? Infrastructure?

It's totally up to them: How they work on that process, whether it's using a certain methodology, whether it's using a certain tool to record it, whether it's Trello cards, whatever.

The individual teams get to decide that on their own, and they have complete autonomy and control over that process.

From a team perspective, we're just making sure that all the metrics we're looking at are transparent and are the closest proxies we have for customer happiness and success. So we don't need traditional things like roadmaps or long, detailed to-do lists.

Of course, it's been a lot easier to implement the customer-driven approach at Drift because we're starting from scratch.

If you're a new startup that doesn't have much process in place, taking on this model is pretty simple. It's not necessarily easy to implement, but it's simple.

Larger companies present more of a challenge because larger companies already have models that they're used to.

And honestly, I don't think many large companies will ever take on a model like this because it's always easier for them to keep pushing on the status quo, and that's usually a top-down, command and control method. So I don't think any of them will be ready for this kind of thing.

When those larger companies look at what we're doing, and how we build teams, all they see are the things on the surface. They see the beanbag chairs and the mural on the wall and the hammocks and all that kind of stuff. And they say, "Alright, I need to get a beanbag chair, and a mural, and a hammock, and if I get that stuff then the team will be productive."

But they're missing the point. They're missing the thing that actually makes it work, which is giving these teams the freedom and responsibility for amazing customers every day.

As the CEO, or a leader within your company, getting out of the way and doing everything you can to support those individuals on your team is the best thing you can do. It's uncomfortable, it's probably not what you're used to, but it's the way that innovative companies have to work today if they want to grow.

My ingredient list for achieving HYPER-GROWTH:

1. Customer-Driven

This is the most important ingredient. The team has to be spending time with customers continually. They need to learn to place the customers needs ahead of their ideas. They also need to consistently WOW customers and increase their product's usage and adoption metrics.

The entire team, especially the tech lead, should spend time with customers each week and shouldn't try to offload this responsibility to the PM or designer because they are "busy." They need to understand that delivering customer value and understanding customers is the best use of their time.

2. Accountability

This is the ingredient that people get wrong the most. They try to have a model of autonomy with very little or no accountability built-in. Remember: Autonomy without accountability is anarchy, not autonomy

Each person needs to be personally accountable for their decisions in order for autonomy to work. Finger-pointing and excuses destroy autonomy.

Because of this, teams should be designed to

be as independent as possible (e.g. they should have a dedicated, not shared, designer).

3. Transparency

The next key is to default to transparency. Individuals and teams need to over-communicate their goals, performance, ideas, and concerns with the entire company via in-person "show and tell" meetings, via the wiki, and via a public scorecard of the metrics they are responsible for.

4. Iterative Approach

After accountability, this is the ingredient that most people get wrong. They interpret being customer-driven as focusing only on major improvements/features. What I have learned is that customers appreciate an incremental approach.

An incremental approach shows customers that you are listening to them and making changes based on their feedback.

It also turns out that most of the biggest impact items you can improve are user experience issues that are preventing a customer from using your product fully.

Don't interpret being customer-driven as being lost in weeks and weeks of customer conversations.

5. Ownership

It's critical that individuals and teams be set up to have clear ownership over a customer-facing product. Most companies get this wrong and always regress to a "pool" model where no one has clear ownership and people work across products on design/backend/frontend tasks.

We need to keep the small independent team model and never let it regress to a "shared" resource model in order for customer-driven autonomy to really work.

Chapter 5

Practical Advice for Becoming Customer-Driven

Learning new habits -- that's the hardest part of becoming customer-driven. And most of that has to happen at the team level.

Engineers, if they're experienced, typically haven't come from environments where they've been communicating with customers. And so that's your first hurdle.

For us, over time, it became part of our culture. So maybe, without even knowing it, we were self-selecting for the kinds of engineers and PMs who enjoyed talking to customers -- so it kept naturally reinforcing itself in the culture.

Communication needs to be central to your organization and your organization's culture. If people aren't communicating, they need to figure out how

When faced with internal communication issues, most companies put Band-Aids into the system.

They add more layers of process. They add project managers. And then they wonder why things are slowing down and why things are not getting done and why they're in meeting hell everyday.

It's because they're not dealing with the root cause of the problem, which is communication.

At HubSpot, we spent a lot of time making sure communication happened. And slowly (these things are slow), people would get it. And they would change. New habits would form, and they would communicate. And eventually the need for those communication Band-Aids would go away and happiness would increase

We built a culture that was happy and that had freedom and that had purpose, and that came from the autonomy and accountability that we introduced. It's simple in theory, but takes discipline.

Separating Product Releases & Marketing Releases

It's a common mistake I see people make: taking the product release and marketing release and making them the same.

This can only lead to disaster.

At HubSpot, we developed this discipline of separating those things, meaning we would release a feature six months before we would ever talk about it from a marketing standpoint.

The reason we would do that is so we would have time for that product to be out with customers -- even if it was a subset of customers.

Depending on the circumstances, we would have 50 beta testers, 100 beta testers 2,000 beta testers, or more. And they'd be using that product, and not only using it, but also becoming successful with it.

And that would give the product marketing team time to go back to those customers so that when we had a marketing launch, we could have case studies, examples, and real data.

The takeaway: With any of your releases, work with marketing so that you always have separate tracks for product releases and marketing releases.

Working With Internal Customers

Under the customer-driven model, engineering teams need to serve both their internal and external customers.

When it comes to internal customers, the key is having engineering teams work with other departments toward shared goals -- and having them be measured on shared metrics.

Let's use support as an example. At HubSpot, we'd have the support team, and we'd say, "Hey support, we want to fix the problems that you're seeing the most. We pledge to do that work, but you need to do the work of organizing and prioritizing what we should be focusing on."

Instead of giving this job to the PM or the engineering team, we would put this on the internal customer.

So sticking with our support example, they would come up with a list of the top call-drivers for certain products. And we'd look at that week-over-week, month-over-month, and the teams had to work with support to reduce these top call-drivers over time.

So we were looking closely at these call-drivers and seeing that they were being reduced. And most of the support call-drivers end up being user experience issues.

Infrequently are they major bugs or outages. Instead it's usually people asking, "How do I do x?" or, "What do I do when x happens?" So there are user experience issues that need to be worked out more than anything.

For another example of an internal customer, let's look at sales.

At HubSpot, sales would be studying their win/

loss data: Which deals did they win, which deals did they lose. Then they'd come up with a list of features and functions that they heard about from the prospects that didn't become customers.

It was sales' responsibility to prioritize those issues and feature requests for each product team, and then we'd commit to work with them to deal with those issues to add those features.

External Customer Metrics

When it comes to our true, external customers, we look at a lot of the standard stuff: Response time of application -- is it getting better over time? Outages for that system: How many critical outages? How many soft outages? How much down time have we had for that app over the last week, month, year?

At HubSpot, for each of the cohorts that we would be looking at, both by plan size and by persona type, we'd ask questions like ...

- What's their frequency of use with different features and functions of that team's products? Is it getting better over time?

- Are our best cohorts using the product more over time? How are they using it?
- What are the best combination of products?
- Are they using the best three features that we see that we think are correlated with lower churn?

So we'd look at those quantitative metrics, and then we'd have more qualitative ones, which included:

- The NPS of that customer segment for that product type
- Feedback that we were getting in-app and outside of that app
- Features and functions they were asking for / ideas that they were submitting and voting up

There were many others that we looked at but this gives you an idea of the metrics we were (and still are) interested in.

Making Customer Research a Priority

Our best insights come from user testing and

customer research. A lot of this has to do with getting into the daily practices of the customer. Some of those practices have some overlap with the product that you're building, but most of them should be you observing customers in their natural state and the natural problems that they're having -- irrespective of the product that you're building.

We would get those insights a lot of the time by visiting customers, which is the best. Because we want to see their office, who sits next to them, if they're in a cubicle, what's in their cubicle, what do they have printed out that's hung on the wall, what does their browser look like, what are their favorites, what's on their desktop?

You just really want to understand, as a researcher, what are they doing? What does their day look like?

And the reason why I care so much about that is because rarely do you get that information when you ask someone a pointed question about features or functions or things that they need.

A lot of the times we found that the information we were getting when we asked customers directly was kind of aspirational: It was things that they thought that they wanted or that they dreamed of, but when we looked at what they actually did each day, in most cases it had zero overlap.

So we learned way more by having those interviews and watching what they were doing, and seeing their daily practice, and seeing how they had to go through five different apps to do something, or download something into Excel.

Excel was gold for us. It's always been for me, building the kind software that I do. As soon as I see a customer or prospect use Excel, I know we're onto something. That's where they're doing something that we can help them do more efficiently.

But it's something that almost no customer is going to tell you about. Because it's so boring to tell someone that: "I download this, I export this, I put it in Excel, and I sort it this way, and I do that, then I put it here, then I do this, then I re-upload it here, then I put it in PowerPoint ..."

Who's going to talk about that? It's so boring. But for us -- who are building software for marketing and sales people -- it's important we know that's what they're doing all day long, even though they're never talking about it.

I have earmarked in my schedule a certain percentage of my time that I'm always out talking to customers and prospects and learning from them. I try to organize these meetings to happen in-person because I want to see the customer in their natural environment.

If I can't get it in-person in their office, then I'll try to do it over coffee, or over a walk, or over lunch, because I want to get them in an environment where their guard is down and we can get them talking about things.

Processing Customer Feedback

Over the years, I've talked to a lot of people about the importance of gathering customer feedback. It's one of the most popular topics that people want to talk about when it comes to startups and building products.

And time and time again, without fail, the same questions come up ...

- After I talk to a customer, what should I do with their feedback?
- How do I make customer feedback action-able?
- How do I cut through the "noise" and make sense of what all these customers are tell-ing me?

Here's the secret: People tend to focus on the wrong part of the feedback. Instead of focusing on the root cause or underlying issue behind the feedback, they focus on the subject of that feedback.

For example, a customer might ask, "How do I integrate this with Trello?" And if people hear that question enough times in feedback across their team, they'll start to say, "We have a Trello problem. OK, let's add Trello features. We need more Trello features. I keep hearing about Trello."

So they'll run and rush to go fix the thing that they think is the subject: Trello.

But if they had used a framework like the Spotlight Framework (the one I'm about to show you), they would've known that they were focused on the wrong part of the feedback, and that they probably didn't need new Trello features.

The part of the feedback that they should've been focused on was when the customer asked, "How do I ...?"

Had they focused their attention there, they would've known that the underlying issue wasn't Trello at all. It was a user experience issue.

The Spotlight Framework

1. User Experience Issues
- How do I ...?
- What happens when ...?
- I tried to ...

2. Product Marketing Issues
- Can you/I ...?
- How do you compare to ...?
- How are you different than ...?
- Why should I use you for/to ...?

3. Positioning Issues
- I'm probably not your target customer ...
- I'm sure I'm wrong but I thought ...

Using this framework, we can see that a question like "How do I integrate this with Trello?" fits into the user experience category. Because clearly the customer already knows that the integration is possible. It's not a discoverability thing. They're not asking if it's possible, they know that it's possible, they expect that it's possible, but they just don't know how to get it done.

In contrast, customers could be asking, "Hey, can you guys integrate with Trello?" or "Can I integrate this part of your app with Trello?" Once again, the important part to focus on here is not the Trello part, it's the "Can you ...?" or "Can I ...?"

And what that tells you is that you have some level of product marketing issue.

Because if you can integrate with Trello, the fact they're asking you that and that they don't know means that they weren't educated properly along some part of the sign-up or getting-started path. (It could've been a features page on the website where it wasn't clear, or it could be that you need to do a better job of calling it out inside of the product.)

So that's how I think about user experience issues vs. product marketing issues. But there's also a third category in my framework: Positioning.

Positioning issues are when someone gives you feedback, and they're usually trying to be nice, and they'll say something like, "I'm probably not your target customer, but ..."

Now, if you know that person is your target customer, there's probably something wrong in your positioning that's leading them to believe they're not a good fit

Another example of a positioning issue might be when someone says, "I'm sure I'm wrong about this, but I thought ..."

And again if what they're communicating is what you're actually trying to get across, but they're unsure, then you probably have a positioning issue there you need to work on.

How to Apply The Spotlight Framework

You can use this framework across your team, whether that's in support, design ... ideally across the entire company.

The main thing is to categorize all of your feedback that you're getting. And then the action can be -- depending on the cadence of your company -- that every week or every month you look at the top user experience, product marketing, and positioning issues that you've categorized using the framework. From there, you can prioritize them and start making progress on them.

The best part about this framework: It's so easy to apply.

Just open up a Google Sheet or an Excel Doc or whatever, and just write things down as you're hearing them and put them into the right categories.

As a final takeaway, we all need to do more listening. But then we need to take it one step further. We need to take what we've heard and categorize it.

So, spend the time to use this framework to categorize the feedback that your'e getting, and then take action and measure the results.

Only by doing this will you be able to take the wealth of customer feedback and turn it into something that's actionable.

Final Thought

Every company in the
world will tell you they are
customer-driven...

They'll believe in the principle. They'll even
have framed posters on the wall about it.
"Solve for the customer."

But after spending 20 years in my career
building and leading SaaS companies, I've
learned that none of that means anything un-
less you actually make the structural decisions
to ensure it.

When I rebuilt the product team at HubSpot
back in 2011, I wanted to see if we could get
beyond slogans and mantras to structure it in
a way that intrinsically placed the customer

ahead of everything else.

I made a few decisions -- in form, process, and culture -- that were designed to safeguard the team against misdirection and ensure that customers remained central.

A recurring product management nightmare that I have is when teams stop being customer-driven -- when we have relapses and start getting inside of our own heads, and start forgetting about the customer, and start inventing solutions to the problems that we see although none of us are the actual customer.

Each time this happens I have to stop us, or stop myself, and remind us all that we're not the customer.

We need to get outside of the building and talk to customers, and we need to ship as soon as possible, because we need to find out how much of what we're building is wrong.

I have this belief that everything that we create and every idea we have is wrong, and we need to get it out into the world as soon as possible to figure out how much of it is wrong and how we can correct it.

The end goal is learning. Evolution is a hugely important part of being customer-driven. Your team needs to be able to move fast enough to make changes based on product usage and customer feedback -- not because something is next on a roadmap.

If you want to keep learning with me, visit the Drift blog (blog.drift.com) and check out my Seeking Wisdom podcast (seekingwisdom.io).

Afterword

by Mike Volpe

When HubSpot acquired David Cancel's company Performable in 2011, it was an incredible milestone. I remember thinking "we now have the best product development team in B2B software."

HubSpot's early years were dominated by tremendous growth through top notch marketing and sales execution. Our vision was so broad that it was nearly impossible to deliver an amazing product or customer experience with the investment we were making in those areas of the business. Growth was through the roof, but annual revenue retention was in the neighborhood of 75%, meaning that if we signed up

$100,000 worth of new customers, those same customers were worth only $75,000 a year later.

It didn't take an MBA from MIT (and actually we had SIX of those!) to know that you can't outgrow that customer churn in the long term. As HubSpot's Chief Marketing Officer, I knew we had to not just satisfy our customers, but delight them, so we could build a truly remarkable long-lasting business driven by referrals and upsells.

Bringing David onto our team in 2011 was a major turning point. He gave the product team a singular focus: the customer. It wasn't just some empty slogan that he shouted -- he made real changes that reverberated throughout the entire company.

While we used to organize product updates into scheduled releases to help our marketing and sales teams, under David's leadership the team instead made rapid product fixes and improvements to focus on getting better product to customers as fast as possible

And while internal stakeholders used to debate

at length what should get added to the product next, under David's leadership we ended the debates and delegated it to him and the product team guided by customer feedback to determine the high priority product updates.

As a result of David's customer-driven product model and the renewed customer focus across the company that it inspired, churn began to drop from both increasing customer satisfaction and growing customer upsells because we had new and better products to offer our now happier customers.

Improving our annual revenue retention from ~75% to ~95% was one of the key metrics we discussed with potential investors on our IPO roadshow, making HubSpot one of the best IPOs of 2014.

Ultimately, David succeeded through giving his team the autonomy to jump in and solve problems and not be hindered by things like roadmaps (to the point where I would ask David for a roadmap as a joke). And it wasn't just the product team that changed after David's arrival -- being customer-driven soon became an integral part of HubSpot's culture and business philosophy. And now it's an integral part of David's new company, Drift.

Today, customers have more products to choose from than ever, and they have access to more information about those products than ever. Being customer-driven is how modern companies set themselves apart. It's not about limited-time offers and one-time deals, it's about round-the-clock dedication to your customers.

I'm sure David's book has helped you to better understand how the customer-driven approach works, and how it can help your company grow.

Your next task: Put what you've learned into action and start amazing your customers. Send us a tweet @Drift and let us know the one big thing you will change after reading the book.

Mike Volpe

CMO at Cybereason, founding team & former CMO at HubSpot, proud investor & advisor to Drift

About the Author
David Cancel

• 5x Founder / 2x CEO

• CEO/Co-Founder, Drift

• CPO, HubSpot
IPO: HUBS

• CEO/Co-Founder, Performable
acquired by HubSpot

• Owner/Founder, Ghostery
acquired by Evidon

• CTO/Co-Founder, Compete
acquired by WPP

• Investor/Advisor/Director to Various
Companies and VC Funds